ROANOKE

THE LOST COLONY

BY KARI SCHUETZ

BELLWETHER MEDIA, MINNEAPOLIS, MN

TM

Are you ready to take it to the extreme?
Torque books thrust you into the action-packed world
of sports, vehicles, mystery, and adventure. These
books may include dirt, smoke, fire, and chilling tales.
WARNING : read at your own risk.

Library of Congress Cataloging-in-Publication Data

Names: Schuetz, Kari, author.
Title: Roanoke : The Lost Colony / by Kari Schuetz.
Description: Minneapolis, MN : Bellwether Media, Inc., [2018] | Series:
   Torque. Abandoned Places | Includes bibliographical references and index.
   | Audience: Ages 7-12. | Audience: Grades 3-7.
Identifiers: LCCN 2016059512 (print) | LCCN 2017000697 (ebook) | ISBN
   9781626176980 (hardcover : alk. paper) | ISBN 9781681034287 (ebook)
Subjects: LCSH: Roanoke Colony–Juvenile literature.
Classification: LCC F262.R4 S38 2018 (print) | LCC F262.R4 (ebook) | DDC
   975.6/175–dc23
LC record available at https://lccn.loc.gov/2016059512

Editor: Betsy Rathburn   Designer: Brittany McIntosh

Printed in the United States of America, North Mankato, MN.

TABLE OF CONTENTS

SEARCHING FOR CLUES

As the wind whips through the trees, you step onto a trail that loops around Roanoke Island. Can a walk through the seaside forest offer answers about this abandoned English **colony**?

Looking for clues, you brush your fingers across a large oak tree. But you only feel bark. There are no carvings in its trunk.

reconstructed
earthen fort

Signs mark your way along the trail. You pause
to read about the area's history. But the signs do
not tell why Roanoke's colonists disappeared.

Eventually, you complete the loop. Then you come to a reconstructed fort. Standing in its center, you wonder what happened to the lost colony of Roanoke.

AN ISLAND SETTLEMENT

Roanoke is where the English first tried to settle in North America. The small island lies off the coast of present-day North Carolina.

Roanoke Island, North Carolina

Small Starter Home
Roanoke Island measures just 12 miles (19 kilometers) long and 3 miles (5 kilometers) wide.

Since 1941, Fort Raleigh National Historic Site has marked the location of the attempted settlement. It has also been the stage for a reenactment play about Roanoke's lost colonists.

The English were not the first people to make a home on Roanoke. Before they settled on the island, Native American tribes had already been living in the area.

Upon arrival, the English did not live as peaceful neighbors to all of the native people. They were friendly with some tribes. But others became enemies.

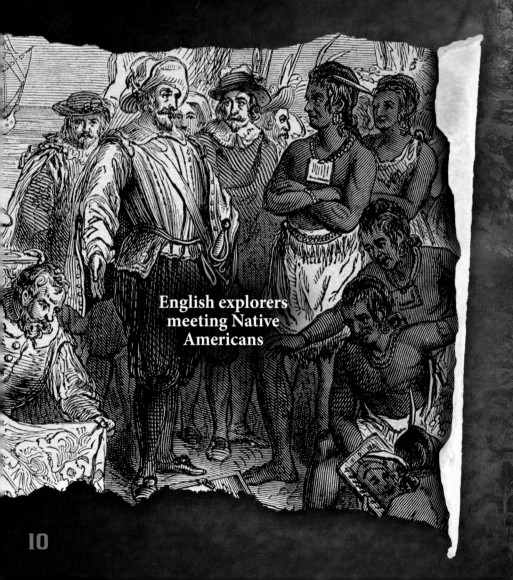

English explorers meeting Native Americans

II

THE FIRST COLONY

In 1584, the first Europeans explored Roanoke Island. With the blessing of Queen Elizabeth I, Englishman Sir Walter Raleigh sent men to the area.

Sir
Walter Raleigh

reconstructed
English ship

His explorers found natural resources
and helpful Native Americans. The next year,
an English fleet set sail to settle Roanoke.
It included 600 men aboard seven ships.

English colonists arriving
at Roanoke

The fleet had a difficult journey across the
Atlantic Ocean. Stormy weather damaged
ships. The needed repairs delayed travel.
Food supplies were also lost.

Soon after arrival, Commander Sir Richard Grenville went back to England for more supplies. About 100 men stayed behind at the settlement. But they soon sailed back, too.

Sir Richard Grenville

ROANOKE TIMELINE

1584:
England sends men to explore the area around Roanoke

1586:
The settlement fails and its men leave

In 1587, more English colonists arrived in Roanoke. The group was made up of 118 men, women, and children.

The colonists had originally planned to settle north in the Chesapeake Bay area. But they ended up staying at the empty settlement. Their governor, John White, led an effort to repair Roanoke.

1590:
The colony is found empty with no explanation

THE DESERTED COLONY

Soon, Roanoke faced problems again. Supplies ran low. The colonists also battled with Native Americans. Governor White eventually traveled back to England for help.

When White returned in 1590, he found Roanoke abandoned. But there were a couple clues. The word *Croatoan* was carved onto a post. And "CRO" was scratched onto a tree trunk.

What did these markings mean? Native
Americans called Croatoans lived near the colony.
Did the colonists move inland with the tribe?

Many theories have formed to explain the deserted colony. Maybe sickness spread. Maybe the colonists starved when food ran out. Or maybe they died in battle against their native neighbors. Will we ever know the truth?

GLOSSARY

bay—an inlet of the sea

colony—a territory claimed and settled by people from a country far away

commander—a military leader

fleet—a group of ships that move together, often for a military purpose

fort—a strong shelter built for protection

governor—the elected or appointed leader of a colony, state, or province

native—originally from a specific place

natural resources—materials in the earth that are taken out to be used by people

reenactment—a performance that uses actors to bring a historical event to life again

theories—ideas that try to explain why an event happened

TO LEARN MORE

AT THE LIBRARY

Blake, Kevin. *Roanoke Island: The Town That Vanished.* New York, N.Y.: Bearport Pub., 2014.

Huey, Lois Miner. *American Archaeology Uncovers the Earliest English Colonies.* New York, N.Y.: Marshall Cavendish Benchmark, 2010.

Rea, Amy C. *The Mystery of the Roanoke Colonists.* Minneapolis, Minn.: Abdo Publishing, 2016.

ON THE WEB

Learning more about Roanoke is as easy as 1, 2, 3.

1. Go to www.factsurfer.com.

2. Enter "Roanoke" into the search box.

3. Click the "Surf" button and you will see a list of related web sites.

With factsurfer.com, finding more information is just a click away.

INDEX

The images in this book are reproduced through the courtesy of: Zack Frank, front cover, pp. 4-5, 11; M. Timothy O'Keefe/ Alamy, pp. 6-7, 18, 20-21; Jeffrey M. Frank, pp. 8-9; H -D Falkenstein/ ima/ imageBROKER/ SuperStock, p. 10; North Wind Picture Archives/ Alamy, pp. 12, 14, 15; jiawangkun, p. 13; Joe_Potato, pp. 16-17; Stock Montage/ Contributor/ Getty Images, p. 19.